Nursery rhymes

Ladybird

Cover illustrated by Suzanne Watts
Published by Ladybird Books Ltd
A Penguin Company
Penguin Books Ltd., 80 Strand, London WC2R 0RL, UK
Penguin Books Australia Ltd., Ringwood, Victoria, Australia
Penguin Books (NZ) Ltd., Private Bag 102902, NSMC, Auckland, New Zealand
3 5 7 9 10 8 6 4
© LADYBIRD BOOKS LTD MMIV
First published in MCMXCIV

Printed in Italy

Hey Diddle Diddle

and other nursery rhymes

illustrated by JAN SMITH

A cat came fiddling
out of a barn,
With a pair of bagpipes
under her arm;
She could sing nothing
but "Fiddle-de-dee,
The mouse has married
the bumblebee."
Pipe, cat; dance, mouse;
We'll have a wedding
at our good house.

Hickory, dickory, dock,
The mouse ran up the clock;
The clock struck one,
The mouse ran down,
Hickory, dickory, dock.

Blow, wind, blow! and go, mill, go!
That the miller may grind his corn;
That the baker may take it,
And into bread make it,
And bring us a loaf in the morn.

Dr Foster went to Gloucester
In a shower of rain;
He stepped in a puddle,
Right up to his middle,
And never went there again.

The north wind doth blow,
And we shall have snow,
And what will poor robin do then?
  Poor thing.
He'll sit in a barn,
And keep himself warm,
And hide his head under his wing.
  Poor thing.

Sally go round the sun,
Sally go round the moon,
Sally go round the chimney pots
On a Saturday afternoon.

Old King Cole
Was a merry old soul,
And a merry old soul was he;
He called for his pipe,
And he called for his bowl,
And he called for his fiddlers three.

There was an old woman
   who lived in a shoe,
She had so many children
   she didn't know what to do;
She gave them some broth
   without any bread;
Then scolded them soundly
   and sent them to bed.

Here we go round
   the mulberry bush,
The mulberry bush,
   the mulberry bush,
Here we go round
   the mulberry bush
On a cold and frosty morning.

This is the way we wash our hands,
Wash our hands, wash our hands,
This is the way we wash our hands
On a cold and frosty morning.

This is the way we wash our face,
Wash our face, wash our face,
This is the way we wash our face
On a cold and frosty morning.

This is the way we comb our hair,
Comb our hair, comb our hair,
This is the way we comb our hair
On a cold and frosty morning.

This is the way we tie our shoes,
Tie our shoes, tie our shoes,
This is the way we tie our shoes
On a cold and frosty morning.

Peter, Peter, pumpkin eater,
Had a wife and couldn't keep her,
He put her in a pumpkin shell,
And there he kept her very well.

Peter, Peter, pumpkin eater,
Had another, and didn't love her,
Peter learned to read and spell,
And then he loved her very well.

Lucy Locket lost her pocket,
Kitty Fisher found it;
Not a penny was there in it,
But a ribbon round it.

Hey diddle diddle,
The cat and the fiddle,
The cow jumped over the moon;
The little dog laughed
To see such fun,
And the dish ran away
with the spoon.

Higgledy Piggledy, my black hen,
She lays eggs for gentlemen;
Sometimes nine and sometimes ten,
Higgledy Piggledy, my black hen.

Two little dicky birds,
Sitting on a wall;
One named Peter,
The other named Paul.
Fly away, Peter!
Fly away, Paul!
Come back, Peter!
Come back, Paul!

Goosey, goosey gander,
Where shall I wander?
Upstairs and downstairs
And in my lady's chamber;
There I met an old man
Who would not say his prayers,
I took him by the left leg
And threw him down the stairs.

Cackle, cackle, Mother Goose,
Have you any feathers loose?
Truly have I, pretty fellow,
Half enough to fill a pillow;
Here are quills,
    take one or two,
And down to make
    a bed for you.

17

Dance to your daddy,
    my bonnie laddie;
Dance to your daddy,
    my bonnie lamb.
You shall have a fishy
    on a little dishy,
You shall have a fishy
when the boat comes in.

One, two, three, four, five,
Once I caught a fish alive,
Six, seven, eight, nine, ten,
Then I let it go again.

Why did you let it go?
Because it bit my finger so.
Which finger did it bite?
This little finger on the right.

Little Bo-Peep
  has lost her sheep,
And doesn't know
  where to find them;
Leave them alone and
  they'll come home,
Wagging their tails behind them.

Mary had a little lamb,
Its fleece was white as snow;
And everywhere that Mary went
The lamb was sure to go.

It followed her to school one day,
That was against the rule;
It made the children laugh and play
To see a lamb at school.

Baa, baa, black sheep,
Have you any wool?
Yes, sir, yes, sir,
Three bags full;
One for the master,
And one for the dame,
And one for the little boy
Who lives down the lane.

Old Mother Hubbard
Went to the cupboard,
To get her poor dog a bone;
But when she got there
The cupboard was bare
And so the poor dog had none.

Oh where, oh where
   has my little dog gone?
Oh where, oh where can he be?
With his ears cut short
   and his tail cut long,
Oh where, oh where is he?

Hark, hark, the dogs do bark,
The beggars are coming to town;
Some in rags and some in jags,
And some in velvet gowns.

Bow, wow, wow,
Whose dog art thou?
Little Tom Tinker's dog,
Bow, wow, wow.

Tom
Tinker's
dog

Girls and boys, come out to play,
The moon is shining bright as day;
Leave your supper,
  and leave your sleep,
And come with your playfellows
  into the street.
Come with a whoop
  and come with a call,
Come with a good will
  or not at all.
Come let us dance
  on the open green,
And she who holds longest
  shall be our queen.

Wee Willie Winkie
　　runs through the town,
Upstairs and downstairs
　　in his nightgown,
Knocking on the window,
　　crying through the lock,
"Are the children all in bed?
　　It's past eight o'clock."

I saw a ship a-sailing,
  a-sailing on the sea,
And oh, but it was laden
  with pretty things for thee.
There were comfits in the cabin,
  and apples in the hold;
The sails were made of silk,
  and the masts were all of gold.

The four and twenty sailors
  that stood between the decks
Were four and twenty white mice,
  with chains about their necks.
The Captain was a duck
  with a packet on his back,
And when the ship began to move,
  the Captain said, "Quack! Quack!"

Notes on nursery rhymes

by Geraldine Taylor (Reading Consultant)

Nursery rhymes are such an important part of childhood, and make a vital contribution to early learning. Collections of nursery rhymes are among the first books we share with babies and children.

Rhyme and word-play stimulate language development and help children to recognise sounds. Feeling and beating rhythm, and joining in counting rhymes encourage early number ideas.

Babies will love to hear you say and sing these rhymes over and over again, and will respond to being gently rocked and jiggled.

Toddlers will love to take part in the actions themselves – with lots of clapping, miming and laughing.

The stories and characters of nursery rhymes will fascinate young children. Encourage them to think imaginatively by talking and wondering together about the people and animals. Nursery rhymes are a wonderful source of ideas for dressing-up and story telling.